# Kinlight
## Homegrown Poems

by
Polly Alice McCann

Flying Ketchup Press Kansas City, Missouri

New Revised Edition

© 2019 Polly Alice McCann, © 2017 Polly Alice

All rights reserved.

ISBN-13:-978-1-970151-99-2

# DEDICATION

This book is dedicated first to my best friend, my hope, light, and life. The person who has helped me the most to find a place called home. Secondly to my mother who is a rescuer and champion of real faith and love.

# CONTENTS

## GREY

| | |
|---|---|
| Jacob's Song | 2 |
| Ash Wednesday Bird | 3 |
| Waiting Tree | 4 |
| Icarus | 6 |
| Easter Basket 2001 | 7 |
| When We Had Little | 8 |
| Redland PA | 9 |
| Easter Again  2004 | 10 |

## SMOKE

| | |
|---|---|
| FireKeepers | 12 |
| To My Daughter | 13 |
| Seed of Fire | 14 |
| Dream Landscape | 15 |
| Sails | 16 |
| Ten Ten | 17 |

## GLASS

| | |
|---|---|
| Shards | 20 |
| Daughter's Dream | 21 |
| Rosemary for Remembrance | 22 |
| Pilgrimage to the Grotto | 23 |
| Paper House | 24 |
| Over the Arch | 25 |
| Egg Moon | 26 |

## VAPOR

| | |
|---|---|
| Stuff | 28 |
| Done | 29 |
| Steam and Vapors | 30 |
| Ghosts in the Chick Peas | 31 |
| Frost | 32 |
| Tattoo | 33 |
| Onions | 34 |
| Valentine | 35 |
| Purple Cabbage | 36 |

## EGG

| | |
|---|---|
| Easter Time 2015 | 38 |
| Cadbury Crimes | 40 |
| Black Walnut | 42 |
| Easter Sweetness 2016 | 43 |
| Like Weeds | 45 |
| Jasper Sky | 47 |

# ACKNOWLEDGMENTS

I'm first thankful to my first reviewer and poetry editor, Heather Patrick. Second for my professor, Jaqueline Briggs Martin who taught me thoughtful editing of my poetry during my MFA at Hamline University. I also have to mention the person who taught me how to study and love poetry, Christine Perrin of Messiah University. I can't forget my first poetry writing professor, Julia Kasdorf who shared with me how to write narrative poetry, something that filled all the gaps in my creative life and helped me find the headspace to finish my undergraduate work in art. Last of all, it was a simple thing like the film, *Julie & Julia*, which inspired me to try a poem a day in 2010. The poetry a day "saved my life" in a way I can only expect poets to understand and which also lead to this book. I have to mention Steel's Used Books where I did my first poetry reading as a poet from this proof of "Kinglight" in April of 2018 and my beta readers Millie Edwards Knottingham and Anita Leverich who encouraged me to continue publishing and writing by being inspired by the proof copies I gave them when I taught college writing at Metropolitan Community College in midtown Kansas City 2016 to 2018. Lastly I thank Madie Mae Parker who told me to "just publish the book yourself" after endless years of sending to contests-- which of course lead to starting *Flying Ketchup Press* and the most extreme joy of publishing other poets.

The cover art is by me in 2016. It's a self-portrait entitled, "Reflection." "When We had Little" 24 x 36 inches and acrylic on Canvas. I wanted to create a piece like Van Gough's missing ear portrait. To show that moment when you sit down and realize you have been serving the wrong "leader" and wasting your time hurrying for all the wrong things. The pocket watch at 3 o'clock symbolizes that there is still time left to finish that good creative work you were called to do.

This is a collection of poetry about becoming visible. "When we had Little" published in the May/June 2015 issue of *Bethlehem Writers Roundtable*. "Jacob's Song" published in *arc*[24], 2015 edition; a literary showcase for the Israel Association for Writers in English (IAWE).

# GREY

Jacob's Song

Searching for a place
I have a name
that's not a curse--
a softer rock, a dream

Send me a ladder
Lift me on wings
Come down and take on human skin
We'll see who's stronger then!

I'll wrestle you and pin you down,
grab your heel
I won't let go
until you answer me

Oh God, if in wrestling
hope and blessing are pinned--
I'll scratch and bite and
holler for a name of my own

I will fight
I will not sit silent
I will scream
to be given a name

Bless me too, Father
Bless me

Bless your name forever

Ash Wednesday Bird

Tall as my grey cat
the Wednesday bird
peers at me
from the rain gutter.

Like the raven,
he brings bad news
there is nowhere to land.

There is no rest,
only water
as far as the eye can see.

I reach into my pockets--
in the left ashes,
in the other, a seed.

What I wouldn't give
for an olive branch,
a hope there was stiffener
for my wrinkled heart
soggy with the grey days.

Waitingtree

Under the largest Sycamore tree
ever to grow in Central Pennsylvania
short of hope enough to climb,
I sat in an abandoned field
waiting for a revelation.

I sucked in the hot October air
filled with mud smells and wished
I knew what I was waiting for.

You saw me under the fig tree
praying for Messiah to come
doubting he ever would.

You stopped me under the willow
to envision trees with leaves
for the healing of the nations.

You heard me muttering under ancient oaks
about how your promises
don't make sense in the heat of the day.

And You found me cowering under a broom tree,
forgetting how your hand fed me
through the raven--
your finger carved water from the rock.

Instead of sitting here dying,
listening to the hum of locusts,
I should walk out,
stand on the plain.

Let your still small voice
carry me back to where I can hear
the sound of the coming rain.

Never let me again forget
you had a tree of your own
on an abandoned quarry.

You were the forsaken stone

killed on a mountain of rejection.
You brought salvation
with your own arm.
Somewhere in the world
is an old tree stump
on whose branches were nailed
the Song of God's own heart.

Somewhere outside a great city
victory was won
that I may sing.

Icarus

Whenever I look at this photograph,
I remember you there,
standing a quarter inch tall
on the edge of a canyon
hazy against the caramel twilight.

The Negev whispers a sigh
but you hold your distance
sacrificing your view
to avoid the edge.

Someday, I think, you will not hold
back. You won't dig in your heels,
but run fiercely,
leap off into the air--
the sun setting your
determined face bronze

as you clutch His feathers in each fist,
you'll fly away grinning like an Icarus
who is certain his father's wings
aren't made of wax. I jump too

only I realize too late, you still
stand on the edge.

Easter Basket 2001

Jesus was crucified today,
and so we vacuum the
green church carpet.

Channel 8 wishes us
a blessed Good Friday.

Jesus was buried so you
don't have to go to work today
but you got paid anyway.

That's grace--like the warning
the police officer gave us
instead of a ninety-four dollar fine.

Jesus rose again from the grave,
and so we get up for the early service
and boil eggs.

And so I give you this Easter basket
with chocolates, and tell you
all my strength comes from this--

Jesus rose again
so all our eggs are double yokes.
For this, I am grateful.

When We Had Little

When we had little, I learned
how to take flour and water then add:

oil,
to make tortillas in the brown glazed
bowl from my potter's wheel days
when I dizzily formed clay for grades.

egg,
to make spring roll wraps
stuffed with bowling ball cabbage
which never fits in the vegetable drawer.

butter,
to make pie crust on Thanksgiving
from the Cinderella pumpkin
growing accidentally in the garden.

soda,
to make angel biscuits
light and whiter than air with the recipe
from the traveling truck show.

milk,
to make white sauce for
seafood pasta casserole without the
seafood.

coriander,
to make manna cakes
out of air and whimsy
when there is nothing else.

sustenance from nothing
blossoms to bread
with only a bowl
I can accomplish anything.

Redland, PA

A sweet smell comes from
the old gas stove in the corner.
Whenever I sit in Pearl Bonner's kitchen
I soak it all in before the dream dissipates.

On the Bonner Farm,
four guards like apostles
mark the edge of the dirt road
between two fields.
But the farmer knows them—
servants to both sky and earth,
the trees perpetually call
the artist to try her hand
the poet his words.

If a farmer ever invites you to walk the road
between his fields, always say yes.
You might become a part of the place--
carry it with you-- the land
remaining and changing you
tilling the soil of your heart.

One day I smelled Pearl's peach cobbler
from half a mile away,
but when I moved a thousand miles
to the edge of Lake Valentine,
and the brown prairie
hardened under the ice for
another long winter, I could not
smell the peaches anymore—

Where were the fields pushing
earth into rows of corn held fast
with rose-colored fingers,
the mocking bird's morning calls–
the two blue poles of the wash line
framing my whole world?

When Jeremy came to St. Paul
to find, Robert Bly, he brought
a little jar of dirt from Redland.

Easter Again  2004

It's Easter gain so I clean the toilet
in case we have visitors.

Laura Croft, Tomb Raider goddess,
wishes us a Happy Good Friday
as she looks for her father
on the 12-inch screen of our TV.

Thankfully we've already found him--
At least we try to believe every day
he took on skin and bone over nine months
only to pop out Son of Man
King of the Universe.

The grave only held him for three days,
woman, two hundred eighty-- in utero

When he left again to give us
something better- his Spirit.

So, on this Easter Sunday
I'm glad. . . no, bursting with joy,
to spend my life with you
being formed by our Father
seeking his Spirit together
while we eat M&Ms
out of baskets filled with eggs.

# SMOKE

FireKeepers--

I abandoned this bowl of dough
flour crusting the white of my wrist,
to tell you that the world is not what you think.

You suppose chefs in nobler times invented
gastronomic creations, dishes where
deboned duck swaddles pressed pastry,
where moon shaped dumplings star.

But I tell you this--
Every woman knows in her breast
that she too with a full creative flame--
inspired by a mostly empty cupboard—
has created marvels such as these.

A woman knows a bit of dough
shaped into a heart covers over
the empty places where
there was not enough.

At sixteen, I made Betty Crocker's
Three Cheese Chicken Casserole
without cheese-- or chicken--
I fed a family of six on faith
and a can of Campbell's soup.

With only a bit of dough
I can make the world.
Women know we have always been
the firekeepers.

Even though a man (centuries hence)
be famed for my invention from one
barren day, I will not forget,
I am Woman.

All things began in me.

To My Daughter

When you hold your baby dolls
tandem to your chest to
breastfeed,
you keep the past.
When you bury a dark stick
in the yard, totem up--
to compost it,
you keep the future.

When you tell the window to
Go up! expecting voice command,
and you scorn my cell phone
for its inability to face time
you live in an age
I thought fiction.

When you play house with me--
I pretend I'm the shy kid at school,
you stroke my face saying,
Don't be scared. It's okay.

Today, you are mother,
I am your child.

Seed of Fire

In the cool garage under the high window's glare,
I pull out peppery black seeds from paper pips--
thin black lashes rimmed in terra cotta
There are mounds of them.

Marigolds.
They sift through my fingers like ashes
their scent rising like smoke, a sweet trust
to their former cingeant glow--

In spring, they sprung from a single pungent packet,
a ring of marigolds to protect my hopes--
just a row or two around the runners,
so, I could make a pot of beans like Grandma's

Summer proved short beans won't climb a pole.
Abandoned by fire, her shutters thrown to the ground
The house, a dead bird with one eye plucked out.

In autumn, the garden greets us, a wild thing with
cucumbers the size of my arm. Marigolds,
profusely plump enough for a Jack to climb,
burn like fireworks from fertile vines.
Blooms of red and yellow colors—a garden on fire.
Our old key quivers in the lock, the door opens.

It's winter. Baby and I trample cold leaves and mud.
I tug an old marigold bush out by her roots,
swinging the reliquary bramble of incense.
A sweet threshing of heads—confetti fills the air—

Seeds stuck to my red wool coat. Seeds in our hair
and on our faces. Seeds over the whole garden.
Seeds of hope and flame. Seeds of survival power.
Seeds for every lost hour.

Dream Landscape

I painted a pink tree for you
on a blue field of corn.
Ashes.
I'm sorry that it's gone
now forever. Lost.
No worries,
paint is cheap.
I can brush in
a world of star fruit
and night shine.
I can paint you
a place where
water is any color
you wish.

Sails

I never knew what love was until
your hair curled under
the blue knit hat you slept in
and wouldn't take off because we
pretended we were sailing and your
sled was a boat that would
take you anywhere-- if you wore a hat,
a hat which made you a man
instead of a baby boy with
new teeth as white as sails.

Ten Ten

This Thanksgiving
I'm thankful for--
my quirky kids
who can sneak down
a half flight of stairs
in tandem
with a blanket
over their heads--
like a Chinese Dragon
on Double Ten,
and my
heart pops
like firecrackers.
I am lucky.

# GLASS

Shards

When the grateful window meets the fireman's axe
the shards lay there all summer
in the crevices, the flowerbeds, the railroad ties

The hired man blows away the leaves and trash,
the shards stay behind-- Oh yeah,
and the cleanup guy steals my rake

I will do it myself, says the Little Red Hen
So with thanks, I grab a broom and
sweep up shards of glass—they tinkle like frost
at its very own holiday party

You guessed it, in winter, I get out the shovel. Under snow
and salt, I feel their cold scrape against the pavement--
Shards, invisible but there—still there

When spring comes, I teach the baby not to put shards
in his mouth. I plant a new rosebush in the front garden--
The water hose washes away the menacing diamond thorns

While the kids ride tricycles in the drive,
I find the evening sun the best time to reflect. Yes,
a different angle each day, another shard lights up in flame

The pile of glass gathers on the low wall washed clean
by the rain--smoky yellow to icy white-- In a Mason jar,
half empty, room for tomorrows shards

They will be found eventually-- by the massaging fingers
of rain— the claws of squirrels, curious worms,
the beady eyes of birds. Shards, the only way I know how,
one reflection at a time

Daughter's Dream

In your dream was a little white dog.
He was sewing himself a little jacket.

You drove a pickle car in a race,
a fox was sneaking around looking for a cake
following a trail of crumbs.

Your mother's day amaryllis is a
Zena Warrior Princess of a flower
two twin red trumpets on a muscled stalk,
your "lily" blooms.
I can't comprehend that kind of
primeval muscle from a cup
of tap water, but I underestimate the seed,
fist-sized, and the sugared sunshine's
fattening powers.

Your snowman is a chaulky chicklet
copy of my taller one its stick arms raised in victory.
You've three rolls of wet snow carried fifty
paces in your two gloved hands.
What I don't get is why you just
throw its head disdainfully
on the ground, but I underestimate the
bigger ball you have ready,
and your creative force of choice.

You're my dream weaver, my race winner,
my warrior seed, my destroyer of rotten
attempts. You will be fine, daughter.

You will be fine.

Rosemary for Remembrance

Daughter,
You left some fairy footprints
to remember you by

You pull our focus
past the weave of the veil,
inviting us to peak into
that invisible haven.

We saw inside the seam,
a place between,
you help us imagine
Heaven.

You remind us
life is about joy,
laughter, love and
remembrance.

You held us briefly,
walked us to the end
of a dark shadow then
flew away into the light.

Pilgrimage to the Grotto of St. Lordres

A palmer's pilgrimage
a small hike, easily forgotten—
like last year's palm branches,
yesterday's dream.

Two candles burned in the grotto,
their tiny prisms shadowed
by the dark womb of the cave.
Hope is the thing with feathers.

Born into the bloom of summer,
kissed by daisies with cornflower eyes,
she was mine.

Born into the ice of winter
my prayer lived and slept
by the light of a sparkling fire
He was ours.

So what did happen at the grotto
after my palmer's prayer for a child?
Nothing at first. 'Til there at the foot
of the mountain knelt a Pieta—Mary
bronzed in the instant of grief,
holding her dead son.

Joy and grief go together,
Mary said, *You cannot have one without
the other.* Desperate, I said, *Yes,
if it's the only way.*

Born into our hour of grief
--asleep in death
she was already gone.
A Rose of Sharon bloomed white
for mourning.

Joy and grief go together, Mary said.
You can't have one without the other.
As a mother, I agreed
to take both.

Paper House

My house is humming,
fans are running,
I think it will take flight--
lift silently its honeycomb walls
and float away into the night.

Walls crisp as paper
and light as wafers
I think it will take flight
Dear angels carry my little one
home, safe into the light.

Over the Arch

I know you are gone,
but when you were here and your words were leaving—
when soft came out cotton candy— You said something...
You looked at my little baby and said,

He's gonna have six kids, isn't he?

Easy as you'd say, "He's gonna have brown eyes."
Maybe you meant something about us six
grandkids, before an unexpected seventh.
That could be it.

But no, I want to take it for truth,
'cause I'd like to think you could see over that arch
of time into a place where I'm the grandmother—
where life continues on, instead of falling away.
It's funny, now that my little boy is talking,
he has imaginary sons or brothers
he sometimes calls them.

You know what they do? They ride in a car together.
They climb ladders, to build houses. They fix trucks—
together. Sure, he is only telling stories, just stories.

But no, I want to take it for truth,
'cause I'd like to think he can see under that arch
of time into a place where we've become a big family,
where life continues on, instead of falling away,
It's sunny, and the trunk of the car is full of tools
to build a good life. Many hands attached
to long arms of people there to help each other.

And my hands inside these old rubber gloves,
under the water in the sink—will come out old
and wrinkled, and full.

Egg Moon

It's Easter at 4:24 am.
The sky is a bruise which
blinds the night train's triple call,
muffles my child's cries,
hushes the wind who knocks to get in,
and wakes the bird when it bumps
the hurrying moon.

The moon, broken in half like an egg
is like me, another Humpty Dumpty
shattered by pride,
her mouth an "O" of surprise
as she lies stunned and breathless
on the black ground.

If I could turn back this twisted tea table
to the one square that led here, I would.
I'd sew up the tear that created this hole,
but how to find enough thread
to stitch back a thousand days?

So I will go forward.
I will let the past blow away,
like so many bits of eggshell.

I will step out of this broken coat,
and run around in my bare little yoke.
Yes, a shell-free life will be dangerous,
but it's better than holding still,
to avoid a broken shell.

# VAPOR

Stuff

Stuff your dreams
at night
to sleep
on edge

Spend the day
in dread to pull
cool dreams
like sheets
over
hopes never
heard

When the quiet
night cooks
light into
dark

syrup
enough
to choke
the sun,

whirls with
the wonder
of honeycombed
words

*Go to sleep*

I am a cricket
chirping
under
the garden
wall…

Don't you
smell it—
the first
frost

Donne

My life is a hilltop

of tall autumn grass
where I planted

an orchard,
a patch of brown straw--
whereI expected to eat

peaches,ripe heads
of grass sway--
whereI intended

summer sweetness.
My tears

are the rain
damp on this grass
worth nothing to anyone.
With the wet strands,
I will weave

a large basket.
Next season
on this patch of dirt,

I will tend new trees.
I will find ripe peaches

hanging whereI pruned

small branches.
My laughter is the rain

on the hilltop where
my ladder can't reach

the tallest branch of each tree.
I will harvest the fruit worth
something to everyone,
and I will carry it home
in this basket made
from past attempts.

Steam and Vapors

Sometimes I forget
this is my promise land.
I hate spring in Kansas City.
It's always five am
and the birds are screaming,

The rain is grey--
my dreams are full of storms
I look at the white, faceless air
and I doubt.

In the midst of two or three
It's the mist I can't see,
Not the white shrift floating by,
but a shift in the reason and why--

How to find light for dark sight
or a light load for a heavy one
that's the real milk I need the most.

Give me a teaspoon of truth
each day, no more, it's
sticky sweetness to fatten my shadow,
wasting away on a diet of lies.

You know, it's crowded in here.
There are too many ghosts.

Would everyone who is not me,
    PLEASE LEAVE!

Hear me shout!
No more vapors, only me

Ghosts in the Chick Peas

There are ghosts
in the chickpeas. They float
in the bowl alongside their brothers—
Filmy coats, their memories
of clouds and sky.

I feel for them, the chickpeas--
I know what it's like to wonder
how many times I'll have
to go under to come out clean.

I know what it's like to be forced
to reconstitute, to become
what you once were or
as close to it as you can get.

And when I'm baptized, I too,
see the ghosts of my old selves
rise up. They ask me what I'd wish
for if I could be born again?

I tell them, it doesn't matter
because their doom is certain
while I, newly alive,
may become any dish
I like.

Frost

When you break my heart
it sounds like someone
walking on snow
the sound of a thousand
crystals' last breath
but what you don't know
is that Spring is coming.

Tattoo

I'm looking for a sign
maybe you are too
like

St. John's Revelation Tattoo

Fruit Tree

Take one sweet and sour life
squeeze it into a two-fingered amber glass
climb out from under one crushing experience
beat it like a drum
find a symbol scrap
fallen by the wayside
slide it underneath skin
peal
repeat

Anchor

Grace is not the gentle drip
after a summer rain
but a gasp of breath
from the nearly
drowned
Grace brought us
to the place we dreamt
by desolation
not by destiny
by drowning
not by boat

Onions

If you don't want to cry
while chopping onions
think sweet thoughts
stand on one foot
hold your chin high with pride
keep your mouth slightly open
squint one eye
purge bitterness from your heart
hold a piece of onion under your tongue
balance another on your head
while you hold your hands underwater
and hide the onion root in another
continent so the evil gasses
which cause tears
may not get to you
and then and only then
you will not cry.

Valentine

A few days back, the stream barbled, tribbed,
sang staccato while sliding under Mooseman Bridge
polishing the rocks with its song.
The summer warblers, all peach and honeyed

answered in song. Today I can't hear the water
over the dead heads.
Where purple coneflowers
used to rocket from their beds, there's these

prick-your-finger-blackened-quill dead heads.
They hum louder, Oh God-- almost a dull roar.
I could trim them, or cut back what has died--
new growth might bloom. I could dig out their roots

to steep them--a tea to keep away winter chill.
Ah, but there is a bird. Look. He is pecking the seeds
ever so slyly. He doesn't want me to see him--
happy for an easy meal, his feathers dark

as their grey stalks. Do I choose glove and blade,
the required price-- scrapes and cuts,
a little blood? No. I'll let it go.
Birds and winter's ice will do their work.

Spring will come again on its own.
You know what I'd like to be? A Mooseman Bridge
from Valentine Nebraska, my beams solid Douglas Fir
grey as smoke, my trusses steal, glazed with rust.

I'd hold a grizzly five tons without bulging a muscle--
over air, water, stone each footstep resounds
my heart splayed out for you to walk across.

Purple Cabbage

Last night Pegasus stamped
open his wings to our left
Cassiopeia kneeled on our right
The pole spins on its axis
as we unwound
beneath their icy breath
free falling up over our terrace

As we spin
we encounter all that we know
falling away--

I'd just like to say
I like it here,
I like it here inside
this purple and white fleshed
core where
there is enough--
where there is
enough.

White dawn,
You, purple cabbage,
opened wide to kiss
the frosty stars--
your dress magenta
like the milky way
won wondrous surprise,

come morning
the praise of small
children who found
your rings
of lusty laughter
a miracle, and forgot
to cry over
the other flowers' deaths.

# EGG

Easter Time 2015

It's time for Easter.
Every year, we act
out the parts again
to remember what was
heavy enough to make
time run backwards
and death lose his grip.
T.S. Eliot says Time,
is an occupation for the
saint-

I know it's acted out
by the lowly. On Maundy
Thursday the workers
at the car wash kneel
like Jesus with a disciple
then dry with white towels
to wash away the grime
from where I've been.

I felt baptized, like the 32
people who were baptized on
Palm Sunday, and the life
guard dunked in too-- in the
the name of the Father, Son,
and Holy Spirit-- which made
thirty-three.

Three-three years Jesus stayed
here. I've seen the places
he walked. The rocks
still look ready to cry out for
Eliot's half guessed Incarnation.

Last Sunday, children waved
palm branches. Early pilgrims,
they shouted they'd love Jesus forever,
a boy asked why his father never
came back from war, if Jesus could.

Tomorrow I will get up and take my

two remaining children to church.
We will wear colors as bright as
the Eggs we will hide in the park
behind our back gate.

The dog will bark, the bridge over
Shoal Creek will solemnly preside,
and we will laugh in the damp
new grass, knowing Jesus
is still alive, and promises
only sunny days in eternity--

knowing one day we will
return to our fathers
if they cannot come to us

knowing the lamb means
we were spared, we are
clean, all is reversed,
and time will have no
hold on us anymore.

## Cadbury Crimes

One a.m. and I steal up to the kitchen.
Above the ceramic fowl
lies the candy bowl
with treats from Easter.
A Cadbury egg tastes
almost as sweet in July.
What is the filling
supposed to be?
And what do they
expect us to do with
little chickee shaped erasers?

I've heard people say that
hate is learned, that
children are born innocent
as pink wicker baskets,
I've heard them say it's
easy to be kind.

But what about the fruit that bore
snake seeds into every stomach
since the beginning of time? If babies
are born to love, then
what need we for grace?
What good forgiveness?
What need to erase?

I've heard people say that
hate is learned, Chicken or the egg?
My kids hate Cadbury
Eggs. I never taught
them that. Just
born that way, I guess.

Getting rid of hate
is like picking egg
shells out of quiche.
You never know where
you will find a bit
that sets your teeth on
edge.

Only one way I know
to pick hate out of
every heart--- a surgeon
who can put us back
together again,
after we have
a great fall

someone who can sew blind,
from the inside.

Takes someone
who knows how
we are made and
who knows what
came first.

The chicken
or the egg.

Black Walnut

The Black Walnut
in front of me
the birds behind
Alyssum clouds
our flowerbeds,
Ivy climbs beside

Roses blush stars
even in November--
Love,
I am here

By paving stones,
between branches

there is space
in my heart

Easter Sweetness 2016

It's Easter again
and I fill eggs
with cotton candy-
flavored candy corn.

Life is like that. You
expect something airy
that melts in your mouth
something astounding
enough for a circus
conductor to announce
but all you get is
hard pellets-from a day
you'd rather forget.

This morning I made
myself an Easter basket.
Why not? It has raw vegan
cookies and two Cadbury eggs

Today we will hear
songs in Swahili at the
Methodist Church
at UMKC. Grandma Twinkie
will sing an anthem in
her red choir robe and
probably tear up under
that rose window glory.

The cousins are coming
because my kids and theirs
both have Easter at their moms
this year.

Life is like that. Divided.
Full of sorrow, and then
suddenly the good days
are like a winning lottery
ticket and you wonder
if everyone hears the
fight song soundtrack

for every small
victory.

I guess Jesus did--
received hardness where he
expected love as light as air.
Received sorrow and divorce
where he expected family.

I imagine his best day
had a victory soundtrack so
that he would remember
who he was fighting for.
I hope he smiled --when
he broke death open like
an egg.

Now we can all choose
sweetness.

I know I am.

Like Weeds

My prayers are like weeds along the side of the path
sprawling canopies of fruitless vines
fiery trumpet bushes announce September
with tiny notes of joy.
Strangling creepers, trees of thorns,

these are my prayers
interrupted by the skither of blue tailed skinks
and the cinching murmur of gnats,
but then maybe those are prayers too.

My prayers are like the weeds along the side of the path
chicory as blue as the sky, Queens Anne's Lace,
purple clover swarmed by drunken bees,
thistledown catching the breeze, deadly nightshade's
orbs of seductive poison.

All these are my prayers
interrupted by this snail, shell skidding over
the path from one false step.
Its former silvery trails of indecision grim,
but then maybe those are my prayers too.

You already know what I'll do--
I throw the snail over toward the creek where
the mud is soft and smells worse than sin
where it can cool off,
hope to revive
to life again.

And there on the bank, I know you'll be there—
You don't hide, I can hear your soundtrack
even though the earbuds
beating percussive.
Nothing keeps out the sound of your crickets
in late summer.

I hear them--
  love    love    love    love
     love    love    love    love

Their pronouncement is the substance
under my feet for fathoms deep,
the infinitesimal oxygen I breathe,
and the rhythm from which I live
and move and have being.

The cicadas are even louder, competing
with the sun for power over power
and they say louder and louder--

   I am

               I am

                         I am.

Jasper Sky

This is who I am
I am the air that cradles each tree
the cavernous black Jasper sky
I am the slice of pie between each spoke
of the rusty wheel, the square arch under
the dude ranch timbers. I am the wicking rim
beneath silver white clouds. I am the last note
of the Blue Jay's grey song, the ever-changing gap
paned by every jamb stop limb on crooked tree
the kinlight through every whiskered head of grain
I am the nook under each gliding wing
the quickening blur of the lightning stripe
The silence after the bending road
Yes, this is me
This is me
This is who I am

# ABOUT THE AUTHOR

POLLY ALICE poet, artist, dreamer says that poetry saved her life. She began writing it after a trip to Israel Palestine where she stayed a night in the Negev with a book for her pillow. She received her MFA in Writing from Hamline University. She has been published internationally: in Naugatuck River Review in the US and arc24 in Tel Aviv. She won the 2014 Ernest Hartmann award from the International Association for the Study of Dreams from Berkley CA for research on the subconscious writing process. She loves to grow basil, paint, and find unexpected adventures. She lives with her family near a creek with wooden bridge in the center of the United States. Kansas City, Missouri-- sometimes called-- the city of fountains.

# GARAMOND TYPEFACE

A Parisian printer, Claude Garamond, brought the first typeface of this kind about in the 16$^{th}$ century C.E during the Renaissance period and at the beginning of his career for King Francis I. Best of all, it was based on the handwriting of the king's librarian, Angelo Vergecio. Robert Slimbach, working with Adobe, set about creating a new version of the Garamond font family in the late 1980s with its elegant antique feel, and not least, an eco-friendly type because it uses less ink.

*If you like reading Polly Alice, she enjoys these poets…*

Pablo Neruda
Julia Kasdorf
Li-Young Lee
Walt Whitman
Naomi Shihab Nye
Marilyn Nelson
Maya Angelou

*Look out for more books by Polly Alice McCann coming in 2020*

Tea with Alice
Doorway to Dreams: How to Live a Creative Life
Pray like a Woman

Flying Ketchup Press to discover and develop new voices in poetry, drama, fiction and non-fiction with a special emphasis in new short stories. We are a publisher made by and for creatives in the Heartland. Our dream is to salvage lost treasure troves of written and illustrated work-- to create worlds of wonder and delight; to share stories. Maybe yours. Find us at www.flyingketchuppress.com

www.ingramcontent.com/pod-product-compliance
Lightning Source LLC
Chambersburg PA
CBHW031502040426
42444CB00007B/1184